Spiritual Legal Rights:
An Introduction

Janice Sergison
Anne Hamilton

Spiritual Legal Rights: An Introduction

© Janice Sergison and Anne Hamilton 2020

Published by Armour Books
P. O. Box 492, Corinda QLD 4075 AUSTRALIA

Cover Image: © Victor Santos / canva.com
MIND_AND_I / istockphoto.com

Interior Design and Typeset by Book Whispers

ISBN: 978-1-925380-19-4

A catalogue record for this book is available from the National Library of Australia

All rights reserved. No part of this publication may be reproduced, stored in, or introduced into a retrieval system, or transmitted, in any form, or by any means (electronic, mechanical, photocopying, recording or otherwise) without the prior written permission of the publisher.

Please note: the spelling, grammar and punctuation used in this book are consistent with Australian and New Zealand English.

Spiritual Legal Rights:
An Introduction

Janice Sergison
Anne Hamilton

Scripture quotations marked NIV are taken from the Holy Bible, New International Version®, NIV®. Copyright © 1973, 1978, 1984, 2011 by Biblica, Inc.™ Used by permission of Zondervan. All rights reserved worldwide. www.zondervan.com The "NIV" and "New International Version" are trademarks registered in the United States Patent and Trademark Office by Biblica, Inc™.

Scripture quotations marked BSB are taken from the The Holy Bible, Berean Study Bible, BSB Copyright ©2016 by Bible Hub Used by Permission. All Rights Reserved Worldwide.

Scripture quotations marked ESV are taken from the ESV® Bible (The Holy Bible, English Standard Version®), copyright © 2001 by Crossway, a publishing ministry of Good News Publishers. Used by permission. All rights reserved.

Scripture quotations marked GNT are from the Good News Translation in Today's English Version- Second Edition Copyright © 1992 by American Bible Society. Used by Permission.

Scripture quotations marked HCSB are taken from the Holman Christian Standard Bible®, Used by Permission HCSB ©1999,2000,2002,2003,2009 Holman Bible Publishers. Holman Christian Standard Bible®, Holman CSB®, and HCSB® are federally registered trademarks of Holman Bible Publishers.

Scripture quotations marked ISV are taken from the Holy Bible: International Standard Version®. Copyright © 1996-forever by The ISV Foundation. ALL RIGHTS RESERVED INTERNATIONALLY. Used by permission. Scripture quotations marked KJV are taken from the King James Version of the Bible. Public domain.

Scripture quotations marked KJV2000 are taken from the King James 2000 Version of the Bible. Used by permission.

Scripture quotations marked NAS are taken from the New American Standard Bible®, Copyright © 1960, 1962, 1963, 1968, 1971, 1972, 1973, 1975, 1977, 1995 by The Lockman Foundation. Used by permission. (www.Lockman.org)

Scripture quotations marked NLT are taken from the Holy Bible, New Living Translation, copyright 1996, 2004. Used by permission of Tyndale House Publishers, Inc., Wheaton, Illinois 60189. All rights reserved.

Scripture quotations marked NKJV are taken from the New King James Version. Copyright © 1982 by Thomas Nelson, Inc. Used by permission. All rights reserved.

Scripture quotations marked TPT are from The Passion Translation®. Copyright © 2017, 2018 by Passion & Fire Ministries, Inc. Used by permission. All rights reserved. ThePassionTranslation.com

Contents

Introduction 1

What Is A Spiritual Legal Right? 6

1   Legal Rights Caused By Personal Sin 11

2   Legal Rights From Generational Sin 21

3   Sins Committed Against Us 29

4   Legal Rights Caused By A Refusal
      Or An Inability To Forgive 41

5   Loss Of Control Over Our Body
      And Soul, And Occult Involvement 47

6   Trauma 51

7   Soul Ties 57

8   Judgments And Expectancies 65

9   Inner Vows 73

10   Covenants 79

11   Sexual Issues 89

Summary 93

References 95

INTRODUCTION

'Make every effort to add to your faith goodness; and to goodness, knowledge.'

2 Peter 1:5 NIV

SOME YEARS AGO I WENT to a training school in prayer ministry run by *ANAZAO Ministries*. It was there I was first introduced to the concept of **Spiritual Legal Rights**.

Prayer ministry is very different from ordinary *intercessory prayer*. It is a Holy Spirit-guided conversation that probes the past in order to understand the pain of the present.

Intercessory prayer is *for* a situation; prayer ministry looks *into* a situation, seeking to uncover ongoing patterns in order to resolve the root cause.

Spiritual Legal Rights turned out to be the single most significant lesson I took away from the school. It opened a whole new realm of ministry and healing to me.

At the time I had been involved in counselling, therapy and prayer ministry for a number of years—both on the giving and the receiving end. I was sometimes puzzled when we had done everything possible to bring about change and healing—including casting out demons—yet people did not seem to get completely set free.

Yes, there was always some healing, and it was often deep. However something often seemed to be lacking. Total freedom was elusive.

So I was already on this journey of personal investigation and healing when I went to the school. After it was over, I spent two full days writing in a large notebook. I headed up the pages with all the **Spiritual Legal Rights** categories, and systematically jotted down every incident I could think of. It was a thorough exercise: person by person, event by event, sin by sin—confessing, renouncing, repenting, forgiving and removing anything from my life and my house that God showed me gave **Spiritual Legal Rights** to the enemy.

Included in this 'house-cleaning' were some demons I sensed the Lord was showing me were hanging around and oppressing me. The change was profound. I felt a significant transformation and, along with it, an increase in my confidence and freedom. A greater clarity in my ability to hear from God resulted.

It also changed the way I ministered to others in my therapy practice. I realised we needed to get this teaching to people who are not able to attend schools or seminars, so they too have tools with which to set themselves and others free.

My pastor and his wife eventually heard me teach on **Spiritual Legal Rights** and asked me to lead a session at our church camp on the topic. My group was the largest—showing the level of interest people had. After the session people from other groups came up asking for copies of my notes. They'd been talking to the group in my session and realised they'd missed something vital.

> *He has given us His precious and magnificent promises, so that through them you may become partakers of the divine nature, now that you have escaped the corruption in the world caused by evil desires. For this very reason, make every effort to add to your faith virtue; and to virtue, knowledge.*
>
> 2 Peter 1:4–5 BSB

God has indeed given us precious and magnificent promises, but sometimes our lack of knowledge inhibits our ability to take hold of them.

As a result of this time at camp, I realised people were desperate for tools, along with the understanding and knowledge to use those tools. It became obvious it was well past time for me to get this written. It was time for action, instead of just talk.

This is not meant to be a heavy piece of work. It's designed to be as simple as possible so it can be understood by any believer who wants to be healed and help others heal. However, it's also intended to be as thorough as I can make it— to cover as much as I've currently gathered together on **Spiritual Legal Rights**. There is always more to learn, of course. The journey goes on!

My special thanks to:

PETER TOTH (ANAZAO) for the original foundational teaching. It encouraged me to think and research as well as apply my findings in my own ministry. At the time of writing, twelve years have now passed, and I remain so grateful to Peter for introducing me to these concepts. They have had such a major impact in my life as well as in the lives of others. I am constantly learning more, asking God for more information, discovering the truth of the proverb:

> *It is the glory of God to conceal a matter and the glory of kings to search it out.*
>
> Proverbs 25:2 BSB

DR CHARLES KRAFT for internet teaching and confirmation on the subject of **Spiritual Legal Rights** as well as the types that exist.

ELIJAH HOUSE MINISTRIES for my very first amazing prayer ministry training. It's so wonderful that this ministry provides an easy way for concepts to be integrated into a very powerful and healing path. Elijah House does not use the same terminology: the training there doesn't talk about removing **Spiritual Legal Rights** but it does refer to dismantling the 'house of sin'—this is effectively the same thing.

ANNE HAMILTON for the suggestion that I write a book; you wouldn't have these pages in your hands except for her encouragement and offer to write a contributing chapter on covenants out of her considerable knowledge, revelation and research. She also added insights on governing vows and conflicting vows to chapter 9. Love you, Annie.

SANDRA SELLMER-KERSTEN for her encouragement and affirmation along the healing journey I have walked through with her. Lots of **Spiritual Legal Rights** were dealt with along the way. She was also the facilitator for the 'heart restoration' that needs to accompany the removal of all kinds of **Spiritual Legal Rights**.

It's not enough to just know about these rights on their own. Both knowledge and heart restoration are needed for the full package.

> 'And to knowledge, self-control; and to self-control, perseverance; and to perseverance, godliness; and to godliness, mutual affection; and to mutual affection, love.'
>
> 2 Peter 1:6–7 NIV

Thanks heaps, Sandy. Love you.

Janice Sergison
Christchurch, NZ
January 2020

WHAT IS A SPIRITUAL LEGAL RIGHT?

DR CHARLES KRAFT DESCRIBES A **Spiritual Legal Right** as: '*something that can give demons an opportunity to enter or harass us, or give them the **right** to remain in us even when we try to cast them out.*'[1]

He teaches that the demon will not leave us while legal rights are not dealt with, but remain intact.

Satan gains many advantages over us on the basis of **Spiritual Legal Rights**. These advantages are influenced and supported by our own *free will choices*.

Peter Toth describes a **Spiritual Legal Right** in these terms: 'It is a currency used between the Kingdom of Light and the Kingdom of Darkness.'

These rights are set up and approved by God. They are the rules operating in His Kingdom. They maintain order and hinder chaos. They promote justice while providing for mercy.

Satan must petition God in order to remove our spiritual covering, and he will take ANY opportunity.

---

1   http://greatbiblestudy.legalrights.php

Spiritual Legal Rights are the ammunition used by Satan to bring accusations against us before God. So often we self-sabotage by handing Satan the ammunition ourselves.

Job 1 and 2

The opening chapters of the Book of Job tell the well-known story of how Satan continually asked God for permission to test a righteous man named Job. God agreed to some of Satan's petitions but He gave very clear parameters and boundaries. Satan was not allowed to step over those limits in his dealings with Job.

Revelation 12:10

> *Then I heard a loud voice saying in Heaven: 'Now salvation and strength and the Kingdom of our God and the power of His Christ have come, for the accuser of our Brethren, who accused them before God day and night has been cast down.'*
>
> (Revelation 12:10 KJV2000)

Peter Toth teaches that everything we do, our actions, our thoughts, our words, our attitudes, things we omit, will either ***decrease*** or ***increase*** the influence of the Kingdom of Light or the Kingdom of Darkness in our lives.

Spiritual Legal Rights given to the Kingdom of Light will result in blessings in all areas of our lives:

- our finances (we will prosper[2])
- our physical health (good sleep, adequate immune system)
- our relationships (harmony, peace, stability, few arguments)

I believe our wellness, our wellbeing, our vitality, our energy and our happiness are proportionate to the number and types of **Spiritual Legal Rights** still operating in our lives.

On the opposite side of the coin, **Spiritual Legal Rights** given to the Kingdom of Darkness will have negative effects in the same areas of our lives. These are referred to as curses, yet they cannot affect us without the existence of a **Spiritual Legal Right** to do so.

If any members of our families (back to the fourth generation) are involved in any way in Freemasonry or any of its off-shoots, a **Spiritual Legal Right** will enable negative fruit to manifest in our lives in the areas mentioned above. This is especially true with regard to our health (heart/lung issues) or our mental health (depression, anxiety, and addictions).

It is very common to find fruit of this kind resulting from involvement by our ancestors in Freemasonry or other cults, philosophies or religions. Naturally the same is true if we ourselves have been involved.

Financial issues can arise when **Spiritual Legal Rights** are still operational in our lives. For example: a spirit of poverty can influence us, resulting in lack of enough money to make ends meet or even put us into serious debt. The **Spiritual Legal Right** that gives this spirit access to our situation can show up throughout an

---

2   To 'prosper' in Biblical terms does not mean to become materially wealthy and so have whatever we desire. It means to flourish in a way that we have enough for our needs and also enough to be generous in giving to others.

entire family line, even though the personal/family income may be quite adequate or above average. It becomes a mystery to everyone that so many individuals in the family are making so much money but everyone is always broke!

> *A curse without a cause will not alight.*
>
> Proverbs 26:2 ISV

In the early 2000s, *ANAZAO Ministries* originally identified seven categories of **Spiritual Legal Rights**. Since then, others have added further categories to this foundational list as God has revealed. This current list comes from a variety of teachers, from other Christians, and from my own personal experience in ministry.

In the illustrations provided, all names, places and identifying data have been changed or disguised to protect privacy and confidentiality except when it is *my* personal story.

1

LEGAL RIGHTS CAUSED BY PERSONAL SIN

WHEN LOOKING AT PERSONAL SIN we need to recognise that different categories exist. The three main types are:

- those we are aware of
- those we are unaware of
- those we are ignorant of

Satan does not really care if we are aware, unaware or just plain ignorant about what we do—the results are the same. He is not fair, he is not a gentleman and he tempts us to turn our lives into a mess. He is happy if that mess is corrosive enough to stop us from moving into our destiny with God. These three categories are paraphrased from teachings by *ANAZAO* and *Elijah House.*

1:   sins within our awareness

We all know what type these are. We give ourselves messages like: 'I shouldn't be doing this,' or 'This will hurt me and my family.' But, despite these prompts from our conscience, we do it anyway. Sins within our awareness cover a wide range like: theft, lies, gossip, curse words, occult activities, dishonour, and speaking negative words over other people.

Just on the last point about negative words: what may appear minor can have terrible long-term effects. For example, a teacher may make the off-hand comment, 'You will never amount to anything.' That comment may still be resonating within a person's spirit decades later and be the **Spiritual Legal Right** at the root of the self-sabotage over their career.

When I was about ten years old, I asked my mum if I could learn highland dancing with my friend. Her answer was: 'Don't be stupid. Big fat things like you don't dance.' To this day I have never danced. In one way this did not harm me—it was not as if my calling in life was to be a ballerina.

However, in another way, immense harm resulted. And that came from my attitude to my mother. I judged her, hated her and just wanted to be out of her house. (Not just over the dancing. There were a lot of other things as well.)

My sinful reactions, my hatred, my condemnation of her, my judgments and unforgiveness all became the basis of **Spiritual Legal Rights** for the enemy to accuse me. For things to go wrong in my life. For things to *not* go well.

> 'Honour your father and mother'—which is the first commandment with a promise—'so that it may go well with you and that you may enjoy long life on the earth.'
>
> Ephesians 6:2–3 NIV

How could I inherit this promise—*that things would go well with me*—while I was dishonouring my mum? Through my dishonour I had handed Satan the **Spiritual Legal Right** to keep me from experiencing the fullness of God's favour.

I have long forgiven my mum but have still never tried to dance. And dealing with the judgments I formed against her as a child has been lifelong and ongoing.

Other sins within our awareness include all sexual sin, addictive behaviours, acting out feelings of anger, violence, murder and so on. Please note: I am not saying *feelings* of anger, but rather **acting them out**.

2: sin outside our awareness

This could be sinful behaviour that we *minimise*. 'Ha ha, I'm such a glutton!' we might say as we shove another piece of cake into our mouths. Or we might say: 'Well, I'm only going to do it just this once.'

It could be sinful behaviour that we *trivialise*. 'It's not such a big deal. Besides a lot of people are doing this much more than I am.'

It could be sinful behaviour that we *rationalise*. 'If I don't do this, things will get worse. Anyway, times have changed so it's not so bad!'

It could be sinful behaviour because of a genuine *blind spot*.

Sin outside our awareness is often the result of pride and self-justification. Another example is the trend for some Christians, including leaders, to dishonour others by swearing—even throwing around the 'F bomb' because we are in 'different times'. Blasphemy too is becoming common.

God says it is sinful. It's dishonour of Him and dishonour of others. It presents Satan with a gift: the **Spiritual Legal Right** for others to criticise and not be silenced. Don't do it!

> *It is God's will that you silence the ignorance of foolish people by doing good... Honour everyone. Love the brothers and sisters.*
>
> 1 Peter 2:15; 17 HCSB

Self-righteousness is often a blind spot. Judging others, self-pity, unbelief and manipulation are all sin that we may not be consciously aware of.

I used to be very self-righteous. I looked down on others because I did not do all the awful things that other Christians did... and that they seemed to get away with so easily. I was proud that I had more sense, as well as more self-control. It took quite a while for me to realise that my pride was just as bad, even worse. In Isaiah 64:6 NIV it talks about all our righteous acts being like *'filthy rags'*.

Even more dire, Ezekiel 33:13 NKJV says, *'When I say to the righteous that he shall surely live, but he trusts in his own righteousness and commits iniquity, none of his righteous works will be remembered.'*

I am thinking here of the sins of manipulation and bitterness. The word for *bitterness* in Scripture is the same as the word for *rebellion* and that is referred to as akin to the *'sin of witchcraft.'* (1 Samuel 15:23 KJV) In the same verse, *manipulation* is linked to *arrogance* and *idol-worship*.

Dictionary.com says manipulation is 'to manage or influence skilfully, especially in an unfair manner.'

I do not believe anyone ever sets out—at least to begin with—to manipulate others. I think it comes from deep wounding, and that some people have had to use manipulation in order to survive. It is a way that some people use to take control of their fear. To give it up feels life-threatening. But, frankly, it STINKS! When I see clients who use manipulation as a way of relating to others, I try to teach them to get their needs met in a much more healthy and direct way. Sometimes it takes a long time.

When I worked in the mental health sphere, some clients acted out as a means to get what they wanted or felt they needed. Their manipulations would include threats and attempts at suicide. Unfortunately some of them died waiting to be found after they posted on Facebook what they were going to do. Their attempts at controlling others had gone tragically wrong. We were deeply saddened because these people had become our friends.

A lady I knew well had an only son. He lived with her and was at her beck and call until he was almost thirty years old. He finally met the love of his life and they got engaged. His mother did everything she could to break the couple up. One afternoon she asked him if he would take her for a drive. He replied that he already had arrangements to go out with his fiancée. The conversation went something like:

'Fine. I'll just stay home on my own ... ... as usual.'

'Oh well. I'll check with my fiancée. She probably won't mind if you come with us, mum.'

'Nope, don't bother. I wouldn't dream of intruding. I'll just have a sleep and it will make the time go faster and I won't be so very lonely.'

The interchange went on like this for a while until the son finally said: 'Ok, I'll see you later then.'

At the mother said, 'All right, I'll come.'

Which she did.

Amazing bit of manipulation! Truly it was an Oscar-winning performance. Unfortunately, such behaviour is all too common.

3: Issues we don't realise are sin

- **Rescuing**

Some Christians are *very* good rescuers. They cannot bear to see anyone sad or in pain. They must fix it! Nurses are good at it too. I was both! There *are* times that, if the situation is serious, a person needs a bit of a hand out and a leg up. But to take over in these circumstances could be depriving a person of growth, development and healing.

Did you know there is more than one word for *burden*? In the Greek language of Scripture, there are different kinds of burdens. One is a crushing weight, as big as a boulder and much too great for a single person to carry. It's a devastating event—like a spouse suddenly leaving for someone else, or the death of a child. These are the times we need to support and hold people up.

The other meaning for *burden* can be translated to mean something like a *daily knapsack*.[3] This refers to the things people need to take

---

3   Henry Cloud, John Townsend, *Boundaries: When to Say Yes, How to Say No*, Zondervan 2008

full responsibility for, in their normal everyday routine. But these are so often the very things they want to off-load onto others. They want to be 'rescued' and so they put out feelers to find a rescuer. They're looking for a Saviour other than Jesus.

And some of us try to fulfil that role. Because we have unhealed stuff in us, and because we need to be needed, we leap into the breach. When this happens, neither party will grow.

I loved something Henry Cloud and John Townsend once wrote. They said there's a good way to handle the situation if someone is going on and on and continually putting out an 'invitation' to us to carry their daily knapsack. It's to say something like: 'Wow, that sounds painful. Keep me up to date. I'd love to hear how you work it out.' This not only gives support and encouragement but it also trusts them to be able to problem solve for themselves.

There are other sin issues we may not be aware of at a conscious level.

- **Independence**

This is the opposite of the problem I've just mentioned. Instead of wanting people to carry our daily knapsack, we can't let them help us even when we've got a truckload of boulders crushing us down. We refuse to let people in, even when help is desperately needed. I was especially skilled at this particular one. But let me tell you, it is fear and pride behind this reluctance. I still struggle with the sin of independence.

- **Idolatry**

We know we're not supposed to worship other gods, but it's so easy to switch off that understanding when we're on holiday. We turn tourist and think that it's ok to visit a temple on an overseas trip. When we aren't aware of the meaning behind the protocols, we can unknowingly offer a **Spiritual Legal Right** to a demon. For example, when we go into a temple and remove our shoes, we are putting ourselves in submission to the ruling spirit of the temple. Sometimes merely crossing the threshold is enough. In such circumstances we need to repent and to renounce our attachment to the demons involved in the temple worship.

Some alternative medical practices, such as reiki, yoga and hypnosis, have the potential to give over **Spiritual Legal Rights** because of their nature. Some such practices have their origins in the occult, some in non-Christian religious rites. Christian teachers often have very long lists of alternative medicines and practices to avoid. I do not agree with all of them. So do your research into the background of any recommended practice, talk to people with discernment and ask them to explain their views and, most of all, *inquire of the Holy Spirit*. By the way, 'Christian yoga' is an oxymoron! Yoga means *to be yoked* and is based in Hindu religion. The exercises are intended to yoke the person to a python spirit.[4]

Books that glamorise witches, vampires and werewolves can seduce us into believing witchcraft isn't so bad after all. Even some of the more gruesome whodunit books can sear our consciences. JK Rowling has done a stellar job teaching our kids about the occult in such a way that it seems harmless and fun. Today, when Harry Potter is all grown up, there are plenty of cute little witches willing to take his place in the imaginations of children all around the globe.

Not every book that features a witch is 'no go' territory. CS Lewis,

---

4   See Anne Hamilton and Arpana Dev Sangamitra, *Dealing with Python: Spirit of Constriction*, Armour Books 2017

for example, in *The Lion, the Witch and the Wardrobe* presented the witch appropriately as a true temptress and heartless villain. Rather it is the books that advocate the use of magic and occult power, presenting them as innocuous and beneficial that are the issue.

So if you have unknowingly ventured into these areas, then use the simple tools that God has given us for removing **Spiritual Legal Rights**: repent, renounce, break soul ties and ask God for cleansing. We'll discuss these more thoroughly later, if you're not sure about them. If still in doubt, ask a mature believer to help you.

I had to repent of reading both the Harry Potter series and the *Twilight* trilogy. These books had been lent to me by child clients in my practice. I justified reading them by telling myself I needed to know what the kids were into! I ignored the fact that both series get darker as the stories proceed. The thing was, I enjoyed them. By the time the kids reach the darker stories, they want to know what happens to their favourite characters. They are hooked.

I had a bookcase full of James Patterson, Patricia Cornwell and Robin Cook novels. They were exciting, well-written and had great storylines. About five years ago the Lord impressed upon my heart to get rid of them because they were mostly murders described in detail. I sensed I did not need to be filling my mind with that kind of material. So I switched to a Christian novelist I enjoyed at the time. However I recently gave those books all away because they were too perfect, saccharine sweet and unrealistic.

Ask the Lord about your reading matter. In fact He loves to be asked about **everything**.

2

LEGAL RIGHTS FROM GENERATIONAL SIN

THE LATE JOHN SANDFORD, THE founder of Elijah House Ministries, was one of the first (if not **the** first) to introduce this subject to his readers in *Healing the Wounded Spirit*[5] as well as to his students in the *Elijah House Prayer Ministry* schools.

In his teaching on this topic he says, 'Sometimes prayer ministers exhaust every trace of personal sin in an individual, only to find great trouble still besetting the person's life and family. The trouble may originate from causes outside a person's own guilt or sinful nature, descending instead through family lines. We call this **Generational Sin.**'

I have often had people who come to me for ministry say things like: 'It isn't fair! How can something my ancestors did cause all this much trouble?'

No, it is not fair. However we are never guaranteed that life will be fair. We live in a fallen world. And although it is not *fair*, it is

---

[5] John and Paula Sandford, *Healing the Wounded Spirit*, Victory House 1985

nonetheless **just**—because we not only reap *sinful* consequences from our family tree, we also reap the *good* from our ancestral line as well. And I am never quite sure why we are so surprised about this. After all, the Bible is full of stories about sowing and reaping passing down a bloodline. The warnings are all there.

The sins that pass from one generation to the next, and that consequently have bad effects in our lives, have a special name in Scripture. They are called **iniquities**. Just a few of the places they are mentioned are:

> *So those of you who may be left will rot away because of their iniquities... and also because of the iniquities of the forefathers, they will rot away with them.*
>
> Leviticus 26:39 NASB
>
> *Our fathers sinned, and are no more; and we bear their iniquities.*
>
> Lamentations 5:7 ESV

There are generational legal rights in everyone's family. Some examples include:

- **Health Issues**

Diabetes, asthma, heart issues and allergies can fall under the category of generational legal rights.

In my family my mother, brother and aunt all had diabetes. My mum lost her eyesight because of cataracts due to diabetes, and also had a leg amputated because of gangrene. I had four grandparents, two parents and a brother who died from heart and circulation issues. I don't know if there was any involvement in Freemasonry by my family, but I have helped with classes and prayer sessions for others for several years, and I believe that all the repenting and renouncing have kept me free.

Talking about family curses… one tragic episode in a family is not necessarily indicative of a curse. Dr Selwyn Stevens from Jubilee Ministries wisely comments along these lines: 'Once is co-incidence, twice is suspicious, more than that look at a curse.'

- **Beliefs and Superstitions**

Just about all of us have an eccentric aunt who can't stop talking about some peculiar notion or other! My mother believed that if you had a bath then went outside, you would get pneumonia. *Especially* if you washed your hair as well. She *really* believed it!

When I worked in South Canterbury where it freezes in winter (sometimes until lunch time) I used to bathe, wash my hair and then walk to work with it still wet. My mum would have been horrified. It took me several months to realise I was not going to get pneumonia, but I was actually thriving! This is a minor example, and quite funny—but some mistaken beliefs go incredibly deep and cause a lot of turmoil to people. The enemy latches on to such beliefs and uses them to empower negative fruit in our lives—fruit such as fear and anxiety.

When a faulty belief cannot be reasoned away, then people need prayer and perhaps even deliverance.

- **Addictions**

Compulsive dependence on nicotine, alcohol, food, exercise, pornography, gambling or any other habit may be the result of generational iniquity. Sometimes the addiction may change from one generation to the next: granddad's alcoholism might morph into dad's drug problem.

- **Sexual Sin**

This is such an important topic that it will have a separate chapter of its own.[6] Incest, adultery, fornication, pornography and obsessive masturbation all have generational outworkings.

- **Freemasonry**

Those involved with Freemasonry, as well as Mithraism and Mormonism—which have Freemasonry roots—leave a poisoned legacy for their descendants. Curses are invoked which need to be undone.

Many people are being set free from the effects of Freemasonry, as knowledge of its rituals becomes more widespread and as it becomes obvious what the spiritual issues are. If you suspect or know there is Freemasonry (or other cults, religions or philosophies) in your family even up to four generations back, you need to be set free. Look for a ministry that specialises in such deliverance.

My friend Amy (not her real name) has given me permission to tell her story of being set free from the effects of Generational Freemasonry. I have now known her for a total of twelve years.

Amy's mother had Freemasonry in her family and her father shared in the curses because he was married to her. They were 'pillars' in a large Pentecostal church and well-respected by many. But Amy says that, as soon as they got home from church on Sundays,

6   See Chapter 11

their personalities changed. Amy was affected by the physical, emotional, verbal and spiritual abuse they dished out. All these can be the fruit of Freemasonry curses—along with domination, control and manipulation.

Remember that 1 Samuel 15:23 links *manipulation* to *arrogance* and *idol-worship*? As well as *rebellion* and *bitterness* to *witchcraft*?

Amy developed Post Traumatic Stress Disorder as a result of a shocking incident at age thirteen which involved her father and the male leaders in her Church. She also developed depression and anxiety—symptoms that remained with her up until very recently.

Amy decided to join a class that focused on getting free from Freemasonry. However the enemy attacked her with fear and lies. She enrolled three times before she actually had the courage to turn up for the class. And that was only because she knew everyone who was attending. She managed her fear and anxiety well, apart from a couple of wobbles. She completed all the reading and renunciations. It was when she came for her individual follow-up prayer session that miracles started to happen. She changed visibly after praying to 'take back' her mind, will and all her body parts (her 'members') from Freemasonry. She clearly renounced her alliance with the demons that manifested... in fact she was stomping around the room, clapping her hands and ordering them to get out! She was also encouraging us to pray in tongues!

It was an incredible change. This was a lady who'd had a major meltdown if the words 'deliverance' and 'tongues' were even mentioned in her hearing. She sheepishly admitted later that perhaps she had thrown the baby out with the bath water!

The difference in her has been amazing. She is indeed taking her life back. She is first to welcome newcomers to church, tell the pastor if she does not believe what he said in his sermon, gets words of knowledge for people and is becoming more and more courageous at sharing them.

This is an ongoing narrative but Satan has done everything possible to prevent Amy from stepping into her destiny. But her courage and readiness to deal with the **Spiritual Legal Rights** resulting from her family's involvement in Freemasonry are heading her fast toward what God has for her.

- **Cults, Philosophies and Religions**

Freemasonry with its hidden occult aspects and spiritual rituals is the perhaps the most common source of generational iniquity for western Christians. However, the teaching of some denominations and cults can give rise to **Spiritual Legal Rights** that pass down the generations. Shunning as practised in some Brethren circles, excommunication as well as the proclamation of anathemas in Catholicism, the holding of funerals for those who have left the 'faith' of their fathers can all negatively impact both present and future generations.

Any denomination where Jesus is pushed aside as Mediator and Saviour and a substitute promoted is laying the groundwork for generational iniquity. The most obvious example of this occurs in Roman Catholicism with Mary and the saints; however there are also adherents to New Age teaching who look to angels for help. And of course there are many churches where the minister reigns and his will, not the will of God, is paramount. Involvement in cults such as Jehovah's Witnesses, Christian Science and spiritualism also lead to generational issues.

This does not even touch on the issue of participation in other religions such as Hinduism, Buddhism, Taoism, Shinto, Islam and neo-paganism as well as all their various factions—each of which impacts subsequent generations in both overt and subtle ways.

But never forget the blessings! A few weeks ago I discovered some photos on my computer. I thought one of them—a black and white shot—was a picture of my niece and nephew. However I was puzzled as to why my niece's hair looked so blonde. I printed it out. Then I saw the names. It was my father and his older sister—taken over a century ago, in 1917! They were about three and five years old. I was amazed at the family likeness. I put it in a frame and set it up on the wall. A friend came to visit and remarked on the lovely photo of me and my brother!

Two weeks later and I cannot stop looking at it. A feeling of warmth rises inside when I think of the generational blessings passed down to me. Because they too are part of the package.

3

SINS COMMITTED AGAINST US

THE ACTIONS AND WORDS OF OTHERS toward us can affect us either positively or negatively. The positive influences are a means of growth, but the negative ones can delay or hinder our development. At worst, they can totally traumatise and almost destroy our lives.

The effects can begin in the womb, often as far back as conception. If a baby is longed for, prayed over, welcomed to the family and raised with love and understanding there is usually not a problem. Of course parents are not perfect and all come with their own issues.

Yet the developmental psychiatrist Donald Winnecott believed that parents only had to be *'good enough'* to raise pretty healthy and well adjusted kids. So all you *good enough* mums and dads, please stop giving yourself a hard time now!

On the other hand, babies who are not wanted, welcomed or loved already have a bad start in life. It's true that babies do not understand what is said, but they soak up every feeling, mood and intention through their little souls and spirits. *And* their hearing is good. Not for the meaning of words but for voice tones and volume.

In the late 1960s I worked in a church-run hospital. Its primary purpose was caring for 'unmarried mothers'—some as young as 13 years old. Back then this was very shameful to the girl, her parents, wider family and community. The girls often had a six month trip away to 'visit an aunt' and the pregnancy was never spoken of again. The adoption would be organised, and five days after the birth the girl would go off to the lawyer's office to sign the papers.

While she was gone the new parents would arrive to collect the baby. Shocking? Yes. Cruel? I've heard it said it was. But we loved the girls, cared about them, and mourned with them... and there was nobody doing it better at that time. Sometimes they would have desperately loved to have kept the baby, but there was no government benefit to help out. In addition, there was major societal disapproval.

The reality was that the girls knew there was no way they could keep the baby. So, to protect themselves, they refused to bond. The baby already felt rejected. Then at five days old the rejection became worse. They got taken away by the adoptive parents. At this time the adoption laws in New Zealand stated that records be sealed and private, so the mothers never knew where the babies went.

The point I want to make is this: as a nurse caring for the babies, I was aware of a truly major difference between a baby waiting to be adopted, and one born to one of the married women who come to the hospital to have their babies. The babies belonging to 'our girls' cried and fussed, gained weight more slowly, and often went rigid when we tried to snuggle them. They also had a characteristic odour. I called it the smell of abandonment and have experienced it many times. Not just at this church-run establishment but in public hospitals as well.

So did the 'girls' recover? They got on with their lives but I believe they carried the grief for a long time. Ten years after this I worked as registered nurse in a major hospital in Auckland. One of the student nurses came up to me one day and asked about where I'd worked in 1969. I named the hospital and asked if she had worked there as well. She said: 'I was one of the girls.'

She had been fifteen at the time her baby was born. She then said that that day was her son's 10th birthday. Her own mum, who had since died, was the only other person who ever knew this girl had a baby. We talked almost the whole shift about her experience. She said she thought about her son daily.

So who was to blame? The girl, for her sin at fifteen? Her boyfriend who was the same age? Her mother for sending her away? The system for making it into a big disgraceful secret?

Probably all of the above. But the girl still suffered long-standing trauma and grief—which most likely still goes on. Unless she has received some specialist help.

Over my last 30 years as a therapist and prayer minister, I have worked with quite a few women who never got over releasing a child for adoption. Sometimes it was 100% their decision. Sometimes it was forced upon them. The results are the same.

I have also worked with many very wounded people who were

adopted. A lot of the time they are puzzled and so are their adoptive families at the level of pain they experience. This is especially true when the parents have given the adopted child everything and loved them with all their hearts. Experience has shown me to *always* look at abandonment issues and to start from the womb—or even before.

My belief is that, in most cases, the child given up for adoption is almost certainly not the only case of illegitimacy in this family line. It tends to be a generational sin. The legacies go on.

But praise God. When that wounded person who was adopted so long ago comes for ministry the flow of the iniquity can be stopped.

About fifteen years ago I was at an event with some of my cousins when one of them suddenly said to my brother and me, 'You two have a half-sister. Your mother had a baby before she was married.'

Wooooooooooooooo! Both my parents had long died by then but I rang my elderly aunt—my mum's sister—and she confirmed it. But it turned out that the half-sister was a full sister. Dad was her father. Mum was pregnant while Dad was away serving in World War II and she tried very hard to raise this wee girl by herself. But she gave up the struggle when my sister was four years old and placed her for adoption. A year later and the war ended; my parents married and had me. I grew up believing I was the first baby. My brother and I found our sister, and we connect three or four times a year. I found out from my sister that she had been doing her own search and discovered there was another child before her when Mum was 18. That little one died.

I believe my mother carried massive grief and pain. Her own mother died when she was 16, she was pulled out of school to take care of her sister, and lost two babies. It all happened between the ages of 16 and 24. There were no counselling services in those days, and I don't believe she ever spoke to anyone about her grief and pain. The effect on her was not good and neither was the effect on me. I don't believe we ever bonded. Knowing her history, I suspect this was most likely due to the vow: 'Don't bond. Babies get taken away.'

I have received healing just in the last few years. But the consequences were deep. I felt so sad for my mum but, by the time I found all this out, she was gone and I couldn't ask her forgiveness for the way I refused to bond... ever! So where did all her wounding begin? I have no idea.

The effects on my sister have been lifelong. She keeps poor health, and has had a lot of things go wrong. She is still angry. Mostly at my late aunt who knew but who never told me about her when my mum died. 'Wasn't my business' was my aunt's response.

Parents can cause trauma in the lives of their children—often unwittingly but sometimes, very sadly, intentionally. Often by things that are spoken.

> 'You should never have been born.'
>
> 'You will never amount to anything.'
>
> 'You should have been a girl.'
>
> 'You're the devil's spawn.'

You might not believe that last one but it's true! Someone actually spoke those very words over their child. The spoken word can go deep into people's personal spirit and cause intense wounding.

When I was a kid I was quite challenging, and received the strap from my mother most days. But the effects of that corporal punishment were minimal compared with the verbal abuse I received from her. Some of her words were true, but delivered in an abusive way. Some of them were lies. I have long forgiven my mother who had shocking wounding and grief of her own. I have also dealt with and released any judgments toward her. But the words had gone so deep it took a long time to replace the lies and be set free.

Other ways we can be traumatised by others include physical, verbal, emotional, sexual and spiritual abuse. All of these change who we are and invade our personal boundaries. Traumatic incidents are more devastating if they happen in childhood, or if they happen *again* as an adult following childhood abuse.

Physical and sexual abuse are usually easy to recognise. Also verbal to some degree. It's easy to find teachings on these so I will not say much about them. Emotional and spiritual abuse, on the other hand, can be quite hard to spot, especially if there are already unhealed traumas.

I want to say a little more about spiritual abuse for several reasons. It is often hidden, can be done in a 'sweet' way, can cause chaos in an individual's life, and also because I feel really strongly about it. It can happen in churches, Christian work places or organisations, and is usually perpetrated by leaders. If it is not the leader initially at fault, then once an abuse situation escalates, the track record of most churches in dealing with the problem is abysmal. Neglect—sometimes to the point of criminal negligence and cover-up—is common.

Oftentimes the classic deny-justify-attack strategy is used to turn the problem around and reverse the roles of abuser and abused. It might be evident that one party keeps changing their story as they fail to remember what lies they've told, but since most of us want to flee conflict, we tend to ignore inconsistencies. Those who practise spiritual abuse are usually very skilled at getting influential people on side.

But it's important to keep in mind they are often very wounded people as well. If not, they would not treat others in a way they'd never want to have happen to themselves. Spiritual abuse always involves power and control over others, and may include domination. Covert manipulation is a given and sometimes overt manipulation as well. Just a few signs of spiritual abuse are:

- You feel confused about things said to you and, when you seek clarification, no explanation is forthcoming. You are made to feel in the wrong for asking that the confusion be cleared up.
- You are accused of being 'rebellious' if you disagree with someone in authority, or ask for more details on a particular matter or even for elucidation of a point in a sermon.
- You are forced to accept a laying-on of hands for prayer or are compelled to receive 'a word' against your will.
- You are silenced and not allowed to defend yourself against unfair accusations.
- You are expected to obey a lot of rules, and are sworn to secrecy about organisational matters.
- You are expected to tolerate actions that keep crossing your personal boundaries.

There are no doubt others you can think of and these do not even begin to cover obvious situations where someone in authority uses their power to sexually abuse another. If in doubt, talk to someone you can trust.

All these things give ground to the enemy and open the potential for **Spiritual Legal Rights** to be established—not just for the abuser but also for the abused. When people feel violated, they are tempted into judgments accompanied by bitterness and unforgiveness. It is not judgments that are wrong but those rooted in hatred and condemnation. These hand **Spiritual Legal Rights** over to the enemy, and result in distancing from God.

Some spiritual abuse can be rooted in witchcraft and will need to be lifted off.

So if you are in a church or organisation where you recognise spiritual abuse is taking place, **get out now.** Seek prayer and have any soul ties cut.

Some people are unsure about getting out, especially when so much of their lives have been invested in a particular church community. But Scripture is clear on this point:

> *What harmony is there between Christ and Belial?*
> *Or what does a believer have in common with an*
> *unbeliever? ... Therefore, 'Come out from them and*
> *be separate,' says the Lord.*
>
> 2 Corinthians 6:15–17 NIV

Let me note in passing that Belial is often mentioned in Hebrew though rarely in English translations—and it is a name invariably used in the context of abuse of all kinds, as well as perversion and travesties of justice.

Quite a few years ago I moved to a small country town to start a new job. I also wanted to find a church to attend. I took advice from some people and turned up for the mid-week meeting at a small Pentecostal church. As the service progressed a lady began a very loud and very long wail. The pastor took her outside and on his return he told us that what we had just seen was a 'demonic display' and she was now ex-communicated. Furthermore he forbade any of us to have any sort of contact with her from that point on—even to hang up the phone on her if she called. I was stunned. But I was also curious, and soon found out the rest of the story from some other Christians I knew.

This lady had a mental illness and had been absolutely stable on her medication. She'd been able to function so well that she'd been in ministry overseas for twenty years. However this pastor had told her he was going to pray for her and she was then to throw away her medication.

She had checked with her husband who was a doctor. He told her *no*, she was not to do it. However this pastor told her that *he* was her 'spiritual authority' and she was to obey him. He ordered her to ditch the medication—and she did. What I witnessed in that mid-week meeting was a severe psychotic break due to the withdrawal of her medication. She actually could have died because going off this particular medication cold turkey was dangerous. Her husband called a colleague who re-established her drug regime and she lived a happy stable life for another twenty-five years—even becoming an elder in her new church.

This is an example of spiritual abuse.

The same pastor took me to task for leaving town for a weekend to have a break. He forbade me to go out of town on Sundays, and I wasn't to talk to the people I had just been visiting. I was only allowed to talk to *him*! I actually thought he was pulling my leg, and laughed at him. He then got angry and told me he was my authority and I had to submit to him. I replied, 'Not any more,' and we parted company.

I am fortunate that I saw his attempts at domination for what they were. I was supported through the time by the very people I had been forbidden to talk to.

Others however have not been so fortunate. They have submitted to this type of abuse for long periods of time, often with very serious results. My friend Amy had suffered spiritual abuse as a child, and then time and time again as she grew up.

She had developed a mental illness, and was not always totally accepted in the churches she chose to attend. After working in the mental health sphere for thirty years, I recognise this aspect of her story as a common one. I hear lots of heartbreaking accounts from clients.

She **expected** abuse and had developed a 'bitter root expectation'. This will be discussed in a later chapter.[7]

Some of her perceptions about abuse may not have been totally based in reality. However, that's not relevant; the extent and severity of the wounding is the same.

Amy has now spent five years in a church where she is valued, treated as normal and is being loved to life. God doesn't want us to be abused but, when we are, He can turn what is meant by the

---

7 See Chapter 9

enemy to harm us into our area of greatest strength. This is what I believe will happen for Amy as she grows into ministry and her destiny.

4

LEGAL RIGHTS CAUSED BY A REFUSAL OR AN INABILITY TO FORGIVE

I ONCE WROTE A SMALL LEAFLET to use with children. These kids were coming to see me for therapy. It was important that they understand about forgiveness. So I needed it to be simple. I just pulled it out again and had a look. The basic principles are reproduced in this chapter.

Unforgiveness—that is, the state of being unable or unwilling to forgive—is a very strong drawcard for demonic activity in our lives. Demonic spirits can attach themselves to us because unforgiveness is the basis of a **Spiritual Legal Right**.

> *Forgive us the wrongs we have done, as we forgive the wrongs that others have done to us.*
>
> Matthew 6:12 GNT

How clear is that? As often as we say the Lord's Prayer, we're invoking a **Spiritual Legal Right** over ourselves. Maybe I need to spell it out since it needed to be spelled out for me. Those words of Jesus are conditional: *if we don't forgive others, we won't be forgiven*. They're just like similar words of His recorded in the gospel of Luke:

> *Do not condemn others, or it will all come back against you. Forgive others, and you will be forgiven.*
>
> Luke 6:37 NLT

My life changed radically when I understood this and began to grasp how important forgiveness is.

When I originally heard the teaching at an Elijah House training school I followed up my very first session with a pen and notepad, making lists of those I needed to forgive. FREEDOM!

I had a lady come to me for counselling who had been sick and sad for a very long time. She began telling me about some bad things someone had done to her a long time ago. Then she said, 'I will *never never* forgive him.'

I asked her where he was now, and she said, 'Oh, he's been dead for twenty years.'

I was very surprised and said, 'Well, I guess you're really punishing him, eh?'

She looked at me with her mouth open, then she laughed. 'Oh, my goodness. I'm the only one who is hurting!'

She was right. Not being able to forgive was making her sad and ill.

A lot of people are hurting because they do not know how to forgive. Often it is because they really do not understand what forgiveness is. Here is what I tell people.

Forgiveness is choosing to let hate and judgment for someone go out of my heart, so I can be well and free.

When we hold onto grudges, about things people have done and said it is like a big ball of poison inside us, that makes our heart (and sometimes our body) sick.

Jesus can help us let it all go and forgive.

In fact, without the help of Jesus, true forgiveness is impossible. John Sandford says that it's so impossible we don't actually ever forgive but we can allow Jesus to accomplish forgiveness in and through us.

LET ME TELL YOU WHAT FORGIVENESS IS NOT

- It is **NOT** saying that what the other person did was ok. It wasn't. Sometimes what they did was really bad and hurtful, and they need to be held responsible for their actions. However God is the one who will deal with them, although sometimes people—like the police—may need to be involved as well.
- It is **NOT** saying we have to be friends again and do things with them. Sometimes people have proven they are not safe to be around. However we can choose to forgive and, at the same time, make a decision not to spend time with them in order to keep ourselves safe.
- It is **NOT** excusing, trivialising, minimising or rationalising the wrong that the other person has done. In fact, when we say things like, 'Well, he didn't know any better,' we're actually excusing the sinful action and avoiding forgiveness. Our hearts can deceive us into believing we've forgiven someone when really we've just avoided the whole issue and

minimised their sin. Forgiveness, by its very nature, says that the other person has done something wrong BUT that we don't condemn them, rather we release them to the judgment of God who is the only one who knows their heart.
- It is **NOT** reconciliation. Reconciliation has two aspects: from one side forgiveness and from the other repentance. (Often there has to be a bit of both on each side.) Reconciliation is the right thing to do if the other person has admitted what they did, repented and apologised (and if they are safe to be around). God does not expect us to put ourselves in harm's way once we've forgiven the other person.

WHY DO WE NEED TO FORGIVE?

Because God commands us to do so. Then we can be forgiven for the things we did wrong. Jesus said:

> 'If you find that you carry something in your heart against another person, release him and forgive him, so that your Father in heaven will also release you and forgive you your faults. But if you will not release forgiveness, don't expect your Father in heaven to forgive you of your misdeeds.'
>
> Mark 11:25 TPT

- **So we can be well and happy**
- **Learning to forgive as a young person forms a good habit. It will be easier as an adult.**
- **Unforgiveness sometimes drives *us* to do the very same things we are upset with someone else for doing.**

I once had a 13 year old come to see me for counselling. She was having a really tough time at the Christian school she went to. Nobody wanted to talk to her and they picked on her and bullied her. She ate lunch by herself every day. She was so sad and angry that she refused to go to school and was thinking about hurting herself.

We had a long talk. She eventually recognised that, while the behaviour of her class mates was hurtful and unkind, her own hate and anger with them was not helpful to her. She then made a decision to forgive—EVEN if she was still going to be lonely. So we prayed about it together. After her prayer of forgiveness she felt a lot better.

But imagine my surprise when she came to see me the following week and told me that the girls in her class started talking to her … *the very next day …* and actually invited her to join in their groups. She found healing by **obeying Christ's command to forgive.**

So what are some clues that we may harbour unforgiveness in our hearts?

- Feeling mad with someone and wanting revenge.
- Avoidance. We do not want them near us.
- We make up speeches: 'If they ever do that again, I'll just tell them…!' (Be honest… I'm not the only one who does this!)
- We may have aches and pains but the doctor says the tests all show nothing is wrong.
- We do not want to eat, or we eat too much.
- Bad dreams.

This is an important topic, so you may like to use the following very simple prayer right now. You can also get someone to help you do this.

> **Lord Jesus,** .... (name of the person) **really hurt me when they** .... (specify what they did).
>
> **I have been holding on to hate and resentment in my heart and this has been making me sad/depressed/angry/ill.**
>
> **Lord, please forgive me for holding judgments and grudges against** ....
>
> **I choose to forgive them right now, and I release them from all my judgments. I ask Jesus to empower these words I have spoken and to accomplish His forgiveness in and through me. And I ask You, Lord God, to bless them in Jesus' name.**
>
> **AMEN**

5

LOSS OF CONTROL OVER OUR BODY AND SOUL, AND OCCULT INVOLVEMENT

OFTEN WHEN WORKING WITH PEOPLE in therapy or praying with them in prayer ministry, the presenting issue can be tracked to an event where there was a loss of control. This might have been literal or it might have been figurative.

It can be for a variety of reasons. The most obvious are if the person has undergone an **anaesthetic,** or perhaps is in a **coma** because of illness or accident. When we are not in control of our mind and body, it leaves an opening for the enemy.

In 2007 and 2010 I had hip replacement surgery. The first time, I wasn't aware I needed to protect myself, and even if I had, I wouldn't have known how to. In the long process of recovery I ended up with quite bad depression. In fact, medical people say a 'post-anaesthetic depression' is quite common.

In between surgeries I attended an *ANAZAO* school and learned about the spiritual openings that loss of control can provide to the enemy. So I was much more savvy and prepared the second time around. I knew the previous scenario did not need to recur.

The day before surgery I asked my friends to pray protection, and for angels to be present in the operating room. When I woke up in recovery, I thanked the Lord for His presence, I asked the angels to keep guarding me, and broke all the body, spirit and soul ties between me and the surgeon, the anaesthetist, the nurses, the technicians, the operating theatre, recovery room, and all equipment. This was when I was still in recovery. (Yes, I believe in overkill!) The difference was amazing. I only needed one dose of post-operative pain relief, then just had Panadol. After three weeks, I was already trying out walking sticks instead of crutches, and jokingly asked my friend if I could borrow her car as I felt like going to the movies! Best of all there was no depression. I have taught this to friends having surgery with equally successful results.

If a friend or family member is in a coma you can protect them and break soul ties for them.[8]

In cases where people are struggling with the complex issues of addiction, it can be more serious if the person is not in full control of their thinking, reasoning and decision-making. **The spiritual openings are HUGELY increased if the addictive substances are alcohol and other drugs** including prescription pain medications used long after the pain is diminished or even gone altogether. When a person is intoxicated or high, the enemy has a legal right to attack their mind which is not behaving in a responsible or cognitive manner.

---

8   See Chapter 7.

Hypnosis can be used as a therapeutic tool or as an entertainment, especially for TV. People are often told it is harmless and you would never do or say anything that you wouldn't normally say or do. **This is not true.**

I did an introductory course once in *neurolinguistic programming* (NLP). In the first two sessions I realised there were extremely manipulative aspects, as when we were taught that certain touches or pressure on the hand at the crucial time could programme someone to believe or think differently. I told the course leader what I felt about it and he shrugged. I never went back.

I also got referred to a hypnotherapist in 1985 for treatment for depression. **God protected me.** I was never able to be 'put to sleep'. In fact the lady was quite angry with me for not cooperating and doing it in the way she was taught. I did not go back again. And I have spent a lot of time repenting for involvement in these things!

People who have been involved in Freemasonry, witchcraft or serious New Age activities may have developed the ability to **astral travel.** This means being able to go in the spirit from place to place and see what others are doing. This is demonic and it needs to be repented of and renounced in order to be free.

Many of the so-called innocent games that people play online or with a board on a table are condemned in God's Word because of their access to the occult and the demonic spirit world. They are very dangerous, even for adults. More particularly so for teens and children. Minds can be taken over and influenced. They can lead to depression, psychosis and even suicide. Some examples of these would be:

- Spirit in the glass (ouija board)
- *Dungeons and Dragons* (or similar)
- Any other role-playing games where the person takes on a persona as if it is actually happening
- Any other occultic activities

If you are under attack either physically, mentally or spiritually **and have been involved in any of the above**, you will need ministry for healing and deliverance. The same is true for anyone you know and love. First, you need to repent of and renounce these activities. A good prayer minister can help with this.

6

TRAUMA

SANDRA SELLMER-KERSTEN DESCRIBES TRAUMA AS: *something that happens to us, that is beyond our control, that causes us to feel intense fear, horror, a sense of helplessness, or something that wounds us so deeply, it seems like we've lost the ability to feel.*[9]

There are many and varied reasons a person becomes traumatised. At the point of trauma a demon can take advantage and enter a person.

Some of the reasons someone could become traumatised could be: a car accident, a bad fall, miscarriage, assault or anything that causes injury, shock, panic or a feeling of helplessness. In my home town of Christchurch, one major reason is earthquakes.

A few years back I'd a bad fall in my kitchen and sustained a spiral fracture of the humerus in my upper arm. So I knew immediately what I had done and also knew as a nurse that, for a

---

[9] For an in-depth and thorough study of this subject I recommend a two day seminar with Sandra Sellmer-Kersten either in person (or DVD-facilitated) called *Healing from Trauma*. It is the best I have attended.

fractured humerus, traction should be applied. I was with it enough to do this. My next thought was that my friend Lia and I had been ministering continuously for weeks doing Freemasonry courses. In fact, we had just returned from an anointed women's camp, where almost every woman was ministered to and received healing in some area. The enemy *did not like it*. So I thought, 'What would Lia do in this predicament?'

I began with letting the enemy know that this was not going to work. **I would not stop helping others get free.** Then I renounced and lifted off all trauma, fear, pain, shock and horror (thank you, Lia and Sandra, for good training) and tried to find a way to get up off the floor to get to a phone.

Now here is a bit of advice... if, for several years, you have not been able to get up off the floor without climbing up a chair and you are limited to one arm... well, then forget it. It cannot be done. I tried for nearly three hours.

So I told the Lord I was going to have to spend the night on the floor, and asked Him and some angels to be with me. And praise God. There was *no pain*. But I was incredibly cold (which took my mind off any pain!) in my summer-weight clothes in Christchurch in August, doors wide open and no blankets. The spare room with lovely warm blankets was only a metre away, but I could not get up to open the door to get them!

So I lay and shivered, and figured that if I was shivering I was not going to die of hypothermia. I had read somewhere that the cold is not life-threatening till the shivering stops! But I had company all night. Jesus was there, and some angels who brought worship songs all night to my mind (and a dog and cat) who stayed on the chair beside me. At 10 a.m. next day I was rescued by a friend (and some cute ambulance officers too!) I healed well because I knew how to deal with the trauma, and keep it to a minimum.

Trauma can also be the result of life-threatening serious illness. I had meningitis at nine years old. Most of the time is a blank in my memory. But one of the nurses later told me that I was 'such a naughty girl that all the nurses on the shift had to come and hold me down to get my regular injections to fight the infection.' Now I realise that, in 1955, this would have meant gowns and masks every time. Very traumatic for a little girl. Especially one who was desperately ill and seeing Donald Duck climbing up the wall. For years I could not tolerate anyone standing by my bed while I was lying down. I had to quickly get up if someone came into my room while I was in bed. When I learned about praying into the trauma about memories of that situation, I found it no longer bothers me.

Trauma is the natural outcome of physical, emotional, verbal, sexual and spiritual abuse.

About 20 years ago I came across one of those 'life changing' books: *Living From The Heart Jesus Gave You.* It was written by a group of therapists from a recovery centre called *Shepherd's House* in the USA.

What I found to be so profound in this writing was that they sensitively separated different types of trauma. They particularly distinguished between **Type A** and **Type B** trauma. Sandra Sellmer-Kersten also touches on these differences in her seminar. For me it answered a lot of questions. I thought I had dealt with most of the bad things that had happened to me, but I realised I was still in a lot of pain. Then I found out a possible reason why: I had a massive pool of **Type A** trauma that had never been addressed.

I am going to list the differences in these trauma profiles but I would also suggest you get a copy of the *Shepherd's House* book. It could answer some of *your* questions. Some of this section may be repetitive, but I hope that will illustrate the issues a little better.

TYPE A TRAUMA

The staff at *Shepherd's House* describe Type **A** trauma as **A***bsence of the necessary good things*. The trauma is not only harmful but hard to detect. When we lack good things, we often have no idea that anything has been absent in our lives or that we've been traumatised by missing out. Here are some of the causes of Type **A** trauma

- **Not** being loved, cherished or celebrated, just for 'being'—especially in our early years.
- **Not** receiving parental love, encouragement or understanding.
- **Not** being given physical signs of love as a child. No (or very few) cuddles, hugs or sitting on a parent's lap. Or none you can recall.
- **Not** being taught appropriate boundaries and limits as a child. This is very confusing for children. They want good, loving, clear boundaries to keep them safe. On the other hand harshly imposed boundaries are just as damaging.
- **Not** having adequate food, shelter, clothing, medical and dental care.
- **Not** having opportunities to grow and develop personal talents, gifts and knowledge.
- In case of parental loss, or adoption, there is major pain due to a perception of abandonment.

Type A trauma can be healed by recognising it, facing the pain and welcoming new love relationships into our lives. This can sometimes feel very risky, but is ultimately very liberating.

TYPE B TRAUMA

Type **B** trauma occurs when **B**ad things happen. Some of the causes could be:

- Physical abuse—including slapping, punching, kicking, hair-pulling.
- Harsh spanking which leaves welts, cuts or bruises.
- Sexual abuse—including inappropriate touching, kissing, intercourse or anal and oral sex, voyeurism and the sharing of adult sexual themes. Such sharing can involve television viewing, computer porn or magazines, as well as talking about sexual matters in front of the children. Or even having sex while the children are in the same room! Yes, it happens!
- Verbal abuse, bullying, name-calling, internet bullying.
- Abandonment by parents; also separation and divorce. Especially if the parents are unable to co-parent in a loving, healthy way.
- Torture, including Satanic Ritual Abuse.
- Witnessing traumatic events such as someone else being abused, accidents, fires, earthquakes, floods and the like.

In March 2019 in my city a major terrorist attack occurred. A gunman entered two mosques while the Muslim community was at prayer and opened fire, killing 51 people and injuring about another 50. There were children among the victims. It was not just the witnesses who were traumatised by this event, the entire city was in pain. It will take a long time before people feel safe again.

All trauma can give a foothold to the enemy. Especially in the areas of fear, panic, pain, terror and un-forgiveness. These consequences of trauma are the means of handing over **Spiritual Legal Rights** to the Kingdom of Darkness.

So if you are wounded because of any type of trauma—**even if it is forgotten, but it is showing its presence by the fruit in your life**—find a good prayer minister who can work with you on these issues and help you get free. It will be life-changing.

PRAISE GOD I can testify to that.

7

SOUL TIES

A BODY TIE, SOUL TIE OR SPIRIT TIE is a connection between ourselves and anyone or anything we have a relationship with.[10] There are healthy and Godly soul ties and, on the other hand, there are unhealthy soul ties.

These unhealthy ties can badly affect people and they have kept many from their destiny in Christ. The term 'soul ties' is not found in the Bible. However, Scripture does talk about 'one flesh' and about being 'knit together'.

Sexual soul ties are the strongest of all. This is great for a healthy marriage relationship where two really do become one. But God never intended for a sexual relationship to be outside of a committed marriage. But, as we know, this is a sinful world, and the enemy has taken full advantage of this. Therefore sexual connection apart from marriage gives a **Spiritual Legal Right** to introduce chaos in our lives.

These **Spiritual Legal Rights** result from fornication—that is,

---
10   Anazao.

relationships where the partners are not married—adultery, affairs, same sex connection, incest, sexual assault and rape.

These are such very strong ties that, even in an abusive situation, they often keep people going back, time and time again. Outsiders may wonder why those being abused don't just 'walk away' but these ties can feel like unbreakable chains.

Even after a situation is over, the ties can make it hard to bond in a new relationship. It seems almost as if the soul keeps on searching and wanting to re-connect to the previous partner. Where multiple partners have been involved, a person can not only feel fragmented but also unable to understand why it seems to be impossible to connect in a healthy committed marriage. This is often resolved when soul ties have been cut and dealt with appropriately.

When I work with people who admit to previous sexual activity outside of marriage, the first order of business is to cut all previous ties to other partners. Preferably by name. This is however not always possible. I have actually worked with people who have had so many partners they cannot remember them all. But God knows who they are, and we ask Him to remember for us. In my experience, this *always* gives a measure of freedom.

Soul ties are not necessarily sexual in nature, however. Soul ties exist within friendships and emotional attachments. An example of Godly soul ties is given in 1 Samuel 18:1–5 where David meets Jonathan, the son of King Saul.

> *After David had finished speaking with Saul, the souls of Jonathan and David were knit together, and Jonathan loved him as himself.*

1 Samuel 18:1 BLB

Then Jonathan made a covenant with David, because he loved him as his own soul.

1 Samuel 18:3 ESV

Here we see a covenant[11] being raised as a result of the knitting together of two souls. In the same chapter we read about the *unhealthy* soul tie that developed between Saul and David. After hearing the people praise David because of his victories in battle, Saul became angry and eyed David jealously from this time on.

Now it is not just other *people* we can form soul ties with in such a way that our spiritual growth is impeded. Ties can also be formed with animals, objects, events, organisations, places and substances. I'm sure this is not a comprehensive list and I would be interested to hear of any other examples.

ANIMALS

We all know of the lovely bonds that we can form with our pets. They give us love and joy. However if our ties to our animals are more important and stronger than those we have with friends and family this could indicate there are some areas that need healing.

I had a beautiful little Bichon Frise called Chloe. She was a little mummy's girl and liked to have me in her sight at all times. She was sweet and gentle and used to sit in my counselling room bringing comfort to traumatised clients. She died quietly in my arms at fifteen and a half years old. I was able to say all the things I needed to her. I couldn't believe all the cards and flowers I received when she died.

---

11   See Chapter 10

My team leader at work gave me a paid bereavement day. ('She's your family, Janne.') All the cards and flowers were set up on my kitchen table for several weeks, along with her photo and her wee box of ashes. Then I felt it was time to put it all away. It was ok.

Three months later I had the opportunity to get my new puppy, Ruby. But before I did that I spent an hour reflecting on and breaking all the soul ties I had to Chloe. Then I was able to love Ruby. Therapy dog she isn't! She gets banished to the kitchen because she thinks people are there for her entertainment!

OBJECTS

Soul ties can also be formed with 'things':

- Your teddy bear and favourite children's books
- Favourite clothes
- Furniture or car. We find out how much we're attached to them when we try to throw them out!
- Artefacts or souvenirs from trips overseas, particularly to Africa or Asia. Unfortunately, these might have demons attached.[12]
- Gifts from relationships that went wrong. I was once given a lovely lamp from a person who proved to be toxic. But I couldn't sleep after I decided to have nothing more to do with her. So someone suggested the lamp needed to be destroyed. That and breaking ties resolved the issue for me.

---

12 It is true that a carving is, in one sense, just a piece of wood or stone. On the other hand, if the carving has been worshipped as a symbol or a representation of a god or goddess, then it is possible for an opportunistic spirit to use the **Spiritual Legal Right** offered by that worship to come and inhabit the carving.

ORGANISATIONS

Sometimes organisations can be unhealthy for us, such as a spiteful workplace. If we leave, soul ties should be cut.

Alternatively it might be a really happy environment—a workplace, church, or club with a real sense of family. However, because of personal circumstances, we need to leave the organisation. Often cutting soul ties with the place we're leaving is the best way to be free in order to give 100% to the new place or venture.

When I was working in mental health facilities, I used to break soul ties at the end of every working shift. I used to cut these off from the people I had talked to, and the organisation itself.

EVENTS

Soul ties may need to be cut to events. Especially if there is trauma involved.

I have already mentioned my experiences with hip replacement surgery and the importance of praying off the trauma and the loss of control. But other events are really important as well. In 2011, my city Christchurch suffered two devastating earthquakes. We are still trying to recover from them. At the time of writing, it's nearly nine years later and our roads are still full of orange cones. Houses and buildings are still being rebuilt and repaired.

I was three hours away on holiday when the first fatal earthquake happened. We felt the effect, even where I was. In Christchurch all power was totally lost. Yet where I was we had all services and, over the next eight hours, we watched it all unfold on live television.

My neighbours in Christchurch did not know what was happening but I did—in close up detail. I checked to see if they needed me back at work but was told to sit tight and keep safe.

A week later I drove home. On arrival I found big piles of liquefaction lining the roads, potholes in the streets and damaged buildings everywhere. Even though I knew, it was still a shock. My house was fine—something to be said for an old 1960s wooden rental, after all! I lost some glassware that took about $10 to replace, and there were some books that fell out of the bookcase. That was it! I was blessed.

Next week I was back at work—at crisis mental health. Over the next three weeks, I listened to countless stories of earthquake trauma. Almost every client had a story.

Not long after, I was having a day off and could not figure out why I'd been so stressed over the previous couple of weeks. I was feeling depressed and not wanting to go to work. After all, I wasn't even there when the earthquake happened. How dare I be affected!

Then I realised I was suffering 'second hand' trauma as a result of what I was hearing from clients at work. I lay on my bed and asked the Lord what was going on, and He told me to break the ties to the earthquake.

So I did that, and the effects were instantaneous. I felt an immediate peace come over me. My strength and energy came back. I never had the slightest problem from then on.

PLACES

A friend of mine went on an overseas missions' trip which she loved. But a year later she came to see me, saying she'd never been able to settle since her trip. We prayed and broke soul ties to the country and the people. She let out a very loud groan, bent double, and said: 'Wow! That was big!'

She immediately felt relief. I've also prayed with people to break soul ties to childhood homes, towns, schools and workplaces. It's powerful stuff.

ADDICTIVE SUBSTANCES

I am convinced that one of the major problems with addictions comes from soul ties to the substances. After all they have been a means of comfort and there can be a bond. Then when it is time to get free of the addiction it is very hard because of the tie. For me it was ice cream. I have been known to polish off two litres in one day! I always told myself it was going to last for the whole week. But it never did. It 'called me' too strongly from the freezer. After I heard this teaching back over ten years ago I broke the ties to ice cream! Then I never bought any for about a year.

Since then I buy some occasionally, but in a *much* smaller container and eat it in a day. It still calls me if it is there, but I no longer 'need' it in my freezer. So how do we cut soul ties? It's actually quite simple.

- Identify any soul ties present
- Confess, repent, renounce
- Break the ties in Jesus' name
- Ask God to send back to the other person or thing any part of themselves that has become part of you
- Ask God to return to you any part of yourself that has become

part of the other person or thing
- Ask God to rebuke any attached demons and to command them to depart
- Ask God to re-attach you in Godly ways to the other, only if it is His will that the relationship continue

8

JUDGMENTS AND EXPECTANCIES

> *See to it that no one falls short of the grace of God and that no bitter root grows up to cause trouble and defile many.*
>
> Hebrews 12:15 NIV

The term *'bitter root judgment'* comes from this passage in Hebrews and the concept was developed by John Loren Sandford, the founder of Elijah House Ministries.

Bitter root judgments are simply condemnations that we make about others in the course of life. They are an immensely powerful force driving the issues and trouble we experience. And they are of course **Spiritual Legal Rights** for the enemy to attack us by using the Word of God against us.

> *Don't be deceived: God is not mocked. For whatever a person sows he will also reap.*
>
> Galatians 6:7 CSB

This is the famous sowing-and-reaping principle. It's a spiritual law. The power of bitter roots is simply that, because we must reap what we sow according to the Word of God, then if we've condemned others, we will continually be harvesting condemnation of ourselves.

Molly[13] spent her childhood being intensely angry at her teachers for never explaining properly. They never spent enough time with her so she could understand what she was supposed to learn. In later life, she found that her bosses were repeatedly angry with her for not giving adequate explanations of what she was doing! When, actually, she had explained appropriately many times!

Molly had a bitter root judgment about people in authority and it came back to bite her. Notice how closely her later experience matches her original condemnation of her teachers.

We not only reap what we sow, we reap *in the same kind* as we sow.

When we *judge* we also develop an *expectancy* attached to the judgment.

For Molly her expectancy as a child was that she'd fail any tests. As an adult, this changed into an expectancy that she'd fail to keep a job.

Out of our *bitter expectancies* about life, our feelings, beliefs and actions produce unhealthy fruit until some healing has occurred. When we have sound expectancies about life, we will generally produce healthy fruit.

BITTER ROOT JUDGMENTS *ARE*:

- **critical condemning verdicts** about people or situations

---

13   Not her real name.

- **sinful reactions** to hurt
- **refusal or inability to forgive** those who have wounded us
- **powerfully able to defile others** with our expectations of how they will behave
- **evidence of the law of sowing and reaping** in operation

BITTER ROOT JUDGMENTS *ARE NOT*:

- the hurtful things that happen to us. **Rather they are the way we choose to sinfully react** as a result of those hurtful things.

SO HOW DOES A BITTER ROOT JUDGMENT WORK?

The most powerful judgments are the ones we made as a child. Present day judging can also produce bad fruit but it is rarely as forceful as the condemnations of childhood.

We soon forget our early judgments but they lie dormant in us until the conditions are 'ripe' for reaping.

When the bitter judgment we have sown comes to fruition and is ready to be reaped, we find one of two things happening:

- we repeat the very same behaviour we judged and condemned in others, usually our parents

OR

- we find ourselves being continually wounded in the same way—that is, we expect it

BITTER ROOT EXPECTANCIES

These are practised ways of thinking and acting that make us expect the worst from both ourselves and others. When relationships and attitudes turn out to be just as we expect, our negative thinking is reinforced and confirmed.

This negative thinking can become so strong that it defiles others. You may actually notice that they are normally quite different in their interactions but, with you, they behave just as you'd expect. If you notice this, check your own heart! The strength of the defilement can be tempting them into sin.

BITTER ROOT JUDGMENTS AND EXPECTANCIES are the most common sins that impact our daily lives.

BITTER ROOT JUDGMENTS AND EXPECTANCIES are the most common sins that separate us from God.

John Sandford once said that 'prayer ministers should look for bitter roots as routinely as a doctor takes a blood pressure.'

My mother had a lot of her own issues and as a result was very critical. Whenever she dropped her criticism, she would then refuse to engage. I saw that as abandonment. Eventually at about 11, I decided to fire her as a mother. I judged her as incompetent. From then on, I looked on her basically as a meal ticket until I could provide for myself.

I eventually managed this at 16 years old. However, I really needed a mother's love. In my early years if motherly people, especially Christians, showed me love I unconsciously saw them as a mother figure. As I felt safe, my pain would begin to come to the surface. Nobody ever actually sat and talked to me about this pain, but instead they would criticise me and turn away. Abandonment all over again, in my view. So I—again—had no choice but to fire them!

Sometimes I even moved towns to get away. I had a list of substitute 'mothers' who had criticised me, abandoned me, and been 'fired'. I eventually realised that sharing my heart was not safe. So I became very self-sufficient and independent. I decided I didn't need anyone.

Then I did an Elijah House school and learned of this teaching on bitter roots. It was the most life-changing discovery of my life. I saw how my strong and bitter judgments toward my mother created a powerful expectancy that I would be treated the same by all 'mothers'. My expectancies defiled them into behaving as I 'knew' they would.

STEPS INTO HEALING

The acronym **A·C·R·O·S·S** might help you remember these six steps.

- ***Acknowledge*** the bitter root judgment.

  I recognised it clearly for the first time at the prayer ministry training school.

- ***Confession*** of sin

  To 'confess' simply means to 'agree', so confession is simply aligning with God's Word about the specific bitter root judgments.

- ***Repentance*** for judging with condemnation

I repented of judgments toward my mum. To repent means to turn around. It's a change in behaviour and attitude. It may not come all at once, but we can declare our willingness to repent of our judgments and asking Jesus to empower the words we speak.

- **Release** the other person to God's judgment.
  When we sit in judgment on another person, we take God's place as Judge. Sometimes the severity of His judgment is tempered by our attitudes.[14]

- **Offer forgiveness**
  I forgave my mum for everything I could think of she ever did to hurt me (or that I perceived so). Again, humanly speaking, forgiveness is impossible. But Jesus is able to accomplish it for us. We have to be willing to give Him permission to do that by simply speaking the words and asking Him to empower them.

- **Strike down your expectancies** and renounce any vows[15] you've made
  Some people like to surrender them and lay them all by faith at the foot of the cross. Others like to nail them to the cross and have them cancelled there.

- **Speak out resurrection life** by praying for new and good fruit. God has been faithful and answered my prayer. It has never happened again since that time.

---

[14] See Proverbs 24:17–18 NIV: 'Do not gloat when your enemy falls; when they stumble, do not let your heart rejoice, or the Lord will see and disapprove and turn His wrath away from them.'

[15] See the next chapter.

Bitter root judgments and expectancies are the most frequent issues I address with virtually all my clients. Dealing with them has been life-changing and healing for them.

9

INNER VOWS

CLOSELY CONNECTED WITH *BITTER ROOT judgments* and *expectancies* are *inner vows.* This concept was also developed by John Loren Sandford, the founder of *Elijah House Ministries.*

WHAT IS AN INNER VOW?

An inner vow is a **promise** we make to ourselves. It's usually not expressed aloud and, even if we think it regularly, we are often unaware of its existence.

These internal promises can become so deeply embedded in our hearts that they defy the developmental process. People can find themselves feeling and behaving as the vow dictates rather than circumstances warrant.

Vows are common to everyone and they can be extremely powerful. Vows made early in life can be especially tenacious. They can refuse change, and take on a life of their own. They are usually difficult to identify and can be troublesome to deal with even after major healing. This is because demons attach themselves to vows and empower them. Not every vow will have a demon influencing it; however it's wise to consider the possibility. If the vows are reinforcing bad habits, and building defence barriers in our hearts as well as causing anger, fears and anxieties, it's likely it is due to demonic pressure.

Deliverance from these demons is so easy once the **Spiritual Legal Rights** in the sinful vows are dealt with. It's a matter of a simple request to God to rebuke them and send them away.

When **Spiritual Legal Rights** are not dealt with, deliverance can become loud, drawn-out and traumatic. Even if the demon leaves, it will come back sooner or later. What it's looking for when it returns is any **Spiritual Legal Rights** that it can use as a point of access.

SOME EXAMPLES OF INNER VOWS:

I'll never trust a woman.

I'll never be like my dad.[16]

I'll never cry.

I'll always dress in designer clothes.

The words *never* and *always* are dead giveaways to the existence of an inner vow.

Some of these internal promises appear 'good'.

I'll always be gentle.

---

16 Because this vow encodes a bitter root judgment, and because we reap what we sow, it may lead us into the exact opposite: we become exactly like our dad.

I will never show anger.

These can appear righteous but, when they are empowered by the flesh, they can hinder what God wants for us, or lead to pride.

CONFLICTING VOWS

I'll always be polite but I'll never obey any woman.

I'll always keep my word, no matter what it costs.

What happens when someone who has made these two vows finds themselves having to work for a female project manager? Their internal conflict can sometimes be so stressful that they suddenly appear to be unstable and unreliable. Previously that person was considered the most dependable and committed worker but, seemingly out of nowhere, they've become a source of abnormal and inexplicable disturbance.

Now these vows might simply be the result of a boy taking on the role-modelling of his father or they might conceal immeasurable pain from childhood experiences. Either way, they need to be renounced before the situation can be resolved.

Conflicting vows are understood in some medical models to be the basis of some mental health issues such as schizophrenia. It is thought that one vow will always involve an internal promise *never to listen*, while the other vow is hidden but will generally relate to a childhood wounding. Until the vow about listening is collapsed, the other cannot be brought to the light.

One vow that has internal conflict actually built into it is a relatively common one: *no matter what happens, I'm damned if I do and* damned if I don't.

GOVERNING VOWS

This concept has been developed by Anne Hamilton.[17] A governing vow is a promise that overarches every other pledge that has been made in the heart. When such an all-encompassing vow exists, it is only possible to deal with subsidiary vows that are not in conflict with the governing vow.

Examples of governing vows:

> *I will never do anything that might trigger the satanic programming.*

This vow had been made early in life by a man who had been ritually abused. Since renouncing the vow was likely to trigger the programming, and since forgiveness and repentance were also likely to do it, it became clear the man had always been conditional in his forgiveness: 'I'll forgive the man who abused me' was the kind of thing he said out loud but his heart was always adding, '... but only if it doesn't trigger the programming.'

The Holy Spirit had to give a very special strategy for this man to be able to safely relinquish this vow.

Outside of such extreme circles, one common governing vow is:

> *I'm always right.*

This enables some Christians to be very gracious and swift to offer forgiveness but to be totally unable to repent. After all, forgiveness

---

[17] She was working with some survivors of Satanic Ritual Abuse at the time. However the concept proved to have much wider application.

says that the other person was wrong. Repentance on the other hand implies: 'I am wrong.'

When a governing vow—or a multitude of smaller vows—strengthens our defences to the point where we develop a veritable fortress of denial, we can develop what John Sandford called *a heart of stone*.

I had developed this and it required painful dismantling, vow by vow. I'm still working on it but it is a very healing and freeing process!

STEPS INTO HEALING

Again, the acronym **A·C·R·O·S·S** might help you remember these six steps.

- **Acknowledge** the vow; recognise it for what it is.
- **Confession** of sin

  To 'confess' simply means to 'agree', so confession is simply aligning with God's Word about sinfulness of the vow.

- **Repentance** for making the vow

  Tell God you're sorry and you want Him to turn your life around. Ask Jesus to empower the words you speak.

- **Renounce** the vow

  Renouncing goes beyond repenting. In effect, it says: 'I am saying an eternal "no" to these words I have spoken over myself.' It is then wise to ask Jesus to empower your words of renunciation.

- **Offer forgiveness**

You may need to forgive people for tempting you to make this vow as well as wounding you. You may need to forgive people for role-modelling a behaviour that you promised yourself you'd copy—or alternatively *never* copy. And don't forget: we don't forgive, it is Jesus who accomplishes forgiveness in us and through us. All we can do is ask Him to empower the words we speak.

- **Strike down** the vows

    Some people like to ask God to send angel axemen[18] to take an axe to the root of the vow and to smash it into splinters. Others like to have recording angels retrieve all copies of the vows, whether on earth or in heaven, and for the Holy Spirit to breathe on them with tongues of fire.

- **Speak out resurrection life** by asking God to rebuke and dismiss any demons

    Ask Jesus to shut the door on them and paint the lintels and posts of that spiritual door with His blood. Pray for new and good fruit.

Then continue to receive ministry and healing as the Holy Spirit directs. There's no need to start looking for vows in an effort to clean yourself. Let the Holy Spirit be in charge of your healing. He knows you better than you know yourself, after all.

---

18   As mentioned in Ezekiel 9:2

10

COVENANTS

Anne Hamilton

SO FAR WE'VE LOOKED AT various kinds of **Spiritual Legal Rights** we can offer to the enemy so that he is justifiably entitled to tempt, test or attack us.

These include:

- sin done deliberately
- sin done without awareness
- sin done in ignorance
- generational iniquity
- sexual sin
- rebellion, domination, manipulation
- occult activity and idolatry
- refusal to forgive
- refusal to repent
- reaction to trauma or loss of control

- soul ties
- bitter root judgments
- bitter root expectancies
- inner vows

Quite a list! Unholy covenants, however, are in the class of their own. They generally cover all of the territory mentioned above plus much more. They also give over more grounds to the enemy than any other **Spiritual Legal Right**.

Most people think of a covenant as just a higher form of contract. It's a lot more solemn and usually involves unbreakable vows. Yes! It does have solemn vows and promises but that's not what makes it a covenant.

Back in Chapter 7, Janice quoted these verses from Scripture:

> *After David had finished speaking with Saul, the souls of Jonathan and David were knit together, and Jonathan loved him as himself.*
>
> 1 Samuel 18:1 BLB

> *Then Jonathan made a covenant with David, because he loved him as his own soul.*
>
> 1 Samuel 18:3 ESV

If we read these carefully, we see what makes a covenant different. It's a knitting together of two souls into one. The essential nature of covenant is *oneness*.

And that's exactly the problem! Unholy covenants bring us into oneness with the enemy. In addition, covenants go on forever. They have no expiry date. This means that they don't end with the death of the covenant-makers. (Remember David looking for someone in Jonathan's family after he'd been killed in battle? This was because David understood that an integral part of his covenant with Jonathan was a promise to protect his family.)

So covenants just keep on going. They involve families for as long as the bloodlines exist—or else, until someone revokes the covenant.

Now most people, on learning about covenants, want all of this oneness with an unholy spirit annulled in the next two minutes. But it's not something to be rushed. It has to be done extremely carefully with the help of the Holy Spirit. There are curses for breaking the covenant.

In fact, some of the curses are probably operational already. Turning to Jesus for salvation would have been a violation of any covenant with an unholy spirit. Violation brings down retaliation and backlash; and revocation brings even more!

So don't start without consulting your Advocate and Counsellor, the Holy Spirit.

Unholy covenants are the biggest problem as far as generational iniquity is concerned. But how do we know if one of our ancestors covenanted with an ungodly spirit?

We know by the evidence we see; by the fruit apparent in our own lives. If we experience constant *constriction* and *wasting* whenever we try to come into our calling, then there's a covenant somewhere.

It's possible we may have raised[19] the covenant ourselves, through:

---

19   The correct technical terms from Scripture for undertaking a covenant are 'to raise a covenant' or 'to cut a covenant'.

- ritual involvement in the occult
- participation in ceremonies with the Freemasons or within a cult
- sexual activity outside of marriage
- participating in worship of an idol through such activities as colouring mandalas, practising yoga,[20] and chanting a mantra during a breathing exercise
- entering a temple in a foreign country on a tour
- sharing of blood in childhood as in swearing blood brotherhood or pledging eternal friendship via a 'witch's prick'

Some of these may seem strange. The last two are generally done in total ignorance.

The basic principle behind the list, however, comes from the resolutions of the Council of Jerusalem.[21] After the early church had convened to decide what aspects of the Jewish Law that Gentile converts needed to obey, the disciples sent a message to them, saying:

> *It seemed good to the Holy Spirit and to us not to burden you with anything beyond these essential requirements: You must abstain from food sacrificed to idols, from blood, from the meat of strangled animals, and from sexual immorality. You will do well to avoid these things.*
>
> Acts 15:28–29 BSB

---

20 As mentioned in Chapter 1.

21 This was the Council where the question of circumcision for Gentile believers was debated and resolved.

All these prohibitions are covenant-related. That would have been clear to first century converts who knew that when you ate food sacrificed to idols, you covenanted with the idols. When you indulged in sex outside of marriage, you covenanted with your sexual partner. When you touched blood, you shared the life of another and thus covenanted with them.

I believe this list spells out the principle. I don't believe it's the final-for-all-time list of restrictions. This is why I've added to the list above. The apostles didn't need mentioning not visiting foreign temples, because that was automatically implied in not eating food sacrificed to idols. Today, however, we need to be clearer about it.

Most people today, however, are totally ignorant of covenants. And most haven't actually fallen into the trap of raising one themselves. The issue for most of us is that we haven't revoked the covenants that our ancestors invoked.

A common covenant that is passed down from one generation to the next is a covenant with Death.[22] Back at an unknown point in history, some of our ancestors lost so much faith and hope that they came to believe that God is not all-powerful or all-loving. In their total despair and anger, they concluded that Death is the strongest being in the universe.

And so they came up with the idea of a totally perverted covenant: they made an agreement with Death to protect their family from itself!

Now certain types of covenants between humans are specifically intended for mutual protection: the covenanting partners pledge to defend each other to the death. The same is true of similar

---

22   Mentioned in Isaiah 28:15

covenants between God and humanity.[23]

It's totally bizarre and back-to-front thinking to expect Death to defend us from itself! But know what? Unholy spirits will take whatever **Spiritual Legal Rights** we offer them. They will trade with us, no matter how unfair the deal is.[24] As soon as this bargain is made, all the family gets is survival. Their inheritance and calling has been forfeited.

If that's how you feel—that for as long as you can remember you've just been barely surviving—then the reason may be that a covenant with Death has come down your family line.[25]

Always always *always* consult with the Holy Spirit about revoking a covenant.

STEPS TO REVOKING A COVENANT

Yet again, the acronym **A·C·R·O·S·S** might help you remember these six steps.

- **Acknowledge** the covenant

    If possible, recognise the 'strong man' who holds the deeds to the covenant and thus has your calling and family inheritance

---

[23] Actually this is not the normal covenant most people think of: the blood covenant. In both these cases, it is a threshold covenant that is about mutual defence. See Anne Hamilton, *God's Pageantry: the Threshold Guardians and the Covenant Defender*, Armour Books 2015 or any of the series *Strategies for the Threshold*.

[24] Remember that the satan is an expert in trade. That is why he was cast out of heaven. See Ezekiel 28.

[25] For more symptoms of a covenant with Death, see Anne Hamilton, *God's Poetry: the Identity and Destiny Encoded in Your Name*, Armour Books 2011 or *God's Pottery: the Sea of Names and the Pierced Inheritance*, Armour Books 2016

legally locked up. Do not insult the 'strong man' or even call him a thief.

- **Confession** of sin

  If you raised the covenant yourself, then confess your own sin. If your ancestors raised the covenant, then ask the Lord to allow you to speak in identificational confession. That is, to confess on behalf of your ancestors.

- **Repentance** for raising the covenant

  If you raised the covenant yourself, then repent of your own sin. If your ancestors raised the covenant, then ask the Lord to allow you to speak on their behalf in identificational repentance.

  Tell God you're sorry and you want Him to turn your life around. Ask Jesus to empower the words you speak.

- **Renounce** the covenant

  'I am saying an eternal "no" to this covenant on behalf of myself and my descendants. It ask Jesus to empower these words and to forbid any retaliation against me, my family, friends, colleagues, loved ones including pets and possessions that I am stewarding for God. I ask God to kiss me with His armour of protection.'

- **Offer forgiveness**

  Forgive your ancestors; forgive yourself for taking so long to revoke this unholy covenant.

  Ask God to forgive you. And also withdraw any judgment your family has made against God that led them into making a covenant with another spirit.

And this is worth repeating again: don't forget that we don't forgive, it is Jesus who accomplishes forgiveness in us and through us. All we can do is ask Him to empower the words we speak.

- **Strike down** the covenant

Ask God to send recording angels to retrieve all copies of the covenant and to place them at His feet. Ask for it to be annulled and for the spirits that have any claim in it to be rebuked.

- **Speak out resurrection life** by asking God to send a sign that the covenant is overturned

This often takes a considerable time. The sign of the breaking of a covenant with Death is an 'unnatural' event in the natural world. The examples given in Isaiah 28:21 refer to the sun standing still and an inland tsunami. I always ask for gentler and less dramatically destructive things!

One last note about **Spiritual Legal Rights** and their connection with covenants and my apologies (but not many! ☺) for the relatively heavy-duty theology to finish this chapter.

The **Spiritual Legal Rights** that are exercised by the enemy over our lives have two sources: one is *ourselves*, the other is *God*. We can negate the **Spiritual Legal Rights** that we ourselves have given over to the satan—and we do this by speaking out words of repentance, renunciation and forgiveness that are empowered by Jesus Himself. However we *cannot* annul the **Spiritual Legal Rights** that have been given to the satan by God.

Most people are shocked to discover that God has actually granted the enemy specific **Spiritual Legal Rights**. The most significant of these rights is found when God pronounces sentence on the serpent in the Garden of Eden.

> *And I will put enmity between you and the woman, and between your seed and her seed. He will crush your head, and you will strike His heel.*
>
> Genesis 3:15 BSB

That last word 'heel' has a double meaning in Hebrew. It is also the word for 'if', and 'if' signifies a *choice*. This verse shows that God granted the satan the right to test our choices.

So our attempts to strip the enemy of this right by 'binding him'—which, in Scriptural context, actually means 'taking out a legal injunction to stop him'—are futile when his **Spiritual Legal Right** comes from the Word of God itself.

We have to pass the tests we are set and do so with honour. One of the most common ways believers hand over **Spiritual Legal Rights** today during spiritual warfare is by abusing, reviling, insulting and dishonouring unholy spirits. Both Jude 1:8–10 and 2 Peter 2:10–12 warn about the consequences of such behaviour.

Don't do it! And, if you have, go apologise to God.

11

SEXUAL ISSUES

I HAVE WORKED IN THE sexual abuse area for over 30 years. Mostly this has been with women and children. In my early years of practice, many of my clients were not Christians. So I frequently get asked similar questions.

Can non-Christians heal from sexual abuse?

Yes, they absolutely can.

When does sexual play in children become abuse?

If there is an age differentiation of two years or more. Or if there is force/bullying/coercion involved. My personal opinion is that many children indulge in sex play during such games as *Doctors and Nurses*. While it is not the best thing for them to be doing, it is wiser to refrain from over-reacting and direct them with an explanation to more healthy activities. Unfortunately there is a lot of sexual abuse going on between children. There is now specialised help for this problem.

Do people who were abused go on to abuse others?

Sometimes they do, but a history of abuse is not an excuse to become an abuser. There always need to be consequences for their own decisions.

My father/brother/grandfather/uncle abused me. Is he safe to be left alone with my children?

NO! Even if there is the tiniest doubt in your mind, don't do it.

What is the incidence of child sexual abuse?

About 1 in 3 girls before the age of 16. The ratio for boys is increasing—or perhaps they are just becoming braver at telling.

What is sexual abuse? How do I know if it's abuse?

Sexual abuse is *always* non-consensual and can cover the full range from touching through to penile, oral, rectal and object penetration. I also include as abuse: sexual talk or jokes, showing children pornography, and adults having sex in the same room as a child, even if the child is asleep. It is *always* abuse if one of them is under 16 years old, even if it seems to be consensual. *A minor is simply not developmentally able to understand the dynamics and give informed consent.*

What if my child tells me they have been abused?

Don't panic! Affirm the child for telling. *Phone the police.* They have teams trained to handle this.

RAPE

Rape is sexual relations of any sort *against a person's will.* Even if the person agrees to have sex and then changes their mind, it is still rape. And it is a crime.

It is statutory rape in New Zealand, for example, if a man or woman of any age has sex with a woman under 16. **Even if she agrees.**

FORNICATION

Any sex outside of marriage is fornication. As long as it is with a consenting adult, even someone else's spouse, it is not against the laws of the land. At least in western countries. But it is against God's laws and, as we have seen, one of His principles is that *we reap what we sow.* Here are some of the possible negative consequences we can reap:

- unwanted pregnancy
- sexually transmitted infections, including cancer of the cervix
- trauma and pain when the cheating is discovered
- strong soul ties, which can be disastrous for future relationships—soul ties not only accumulate, they are covenantal in nature; the more 'partners', the more tangled the ties.

God never intended the sex act to be a recreational sport

RITUAL ABUSE

Very briefly, this is an increasingly prevalent and serious form of abuse. Or it may be that we are just getting better at spotting it.

I recently started advanced training in this area, and have become more and more shocked as the course has gone along. And I thought I was unshockable! This form of abuse can include mind control and programming. It is extremely difficult to bring healing without specialised ministry from people trained in this area. Ritual Abuse will frequently, but not always, apply to people who have Freemasonry or cult activity in their families.

So if you have received a lot of ministry and are not free despite doing everything you can think of, consider this as a possibility.

Whenever any sin of a sexual nature occurs which also involves ceremonial ritual, covenants will also be in the mix. Take care to go to a professional if you suspect Ritual Abuse because of the possibility of triggering programming or backlash.

Spiritual Legal Rights are not matters to cause fear. In fact, as we become more informed about them, they are a cause for rejoicing. Satan is a legalist. And that's actually a wonderful thing. Because when we remove the grounds for the **Spiritual Legal Rights** he's using to undermine us, he can be dismissed. Imagine if that were not the case. Imagine if repentance, forgiveness and renunciation made no difference in our lives at all!

But, thanks be to God, that's not the case. Amen!

> *Thanks be to God, who always leads us triumphantly as captives in Christ and through us spreads everywhere the fragrance of the knowledge of Him.*
>
> 2 Corinthians 2:14 BSB

SUMMARY

As previously stated, this work is an overview to educate Christians on the concept of **Spiritual Legal Rights**. It is not a healing book, or even a 'how to' book (though it contains many basic principles for healing). It's primarily a 'what' book, to explain what **Spiritual Legal Rights** are and what tools can be used to deal with them.

I have a passion to see people healed and set free. If this little book helps in even a very small way, then it is serving its purpose in the Kingdom.

Janice Sergison
Dip Psychotherapy
Dip Gestalt psychotherapy
MA (Christian Counselling)
Integrated Inner Healing Therapist
Christchurch
January 2020

REFERENCES

CLOUD Henry, **TOWNSEND** John, *Boundaries: When to Say Yes, How to Say No*, Zondervan 2008

HAMILTON Anne: *God's Pageantry: the Threshold Guardians and the Covenant Defender*, Armour Books 2015

HAMILTON Anne: *God's Poetry: the Identity and Destiny Encoded in Your Name*, Armour Books 2011

HAMILTON Anne: *God's Pottery: the Sea of Names and the Pierced Inheritance*, Armour Books 2016

HAMILTON Anne, **SANGAMITRA** Arpana Dev: *Dealing with Python: Spirit of Constriction*, Armour Books 2017

SANDFORD John Loren, **SANDFORD** Paula: *Transformation of the Inner Man*, Victory House Publishers 1982

SANDFORD John Loren, **SANDFORD** Paula: *Healing the Wounded Spirit*, Victory House 1985

SELLMER-KERSTEN Sandra: *Healing from Trauma Manual*

SHEPHERDS HOUSE USA: *Living From The Heart Jesus Gave You*, Shepherd's House Inc 2002

STEVENS Selwyn: *Unmasking Freemasonry*, Jubilee Ministries NZ

TOTH Peter: *Cutting Edge School*, ANAZAO ministries, Australia.

WINNICOT Donald: *The Good Enough Mother* 1953

www.ingramcontent.com/pod-product-compliance
Lightning Source LLC
Chambersburg PA
CBHW071018080526
44587CB00015B/2420